Rats

by E. Sandy Powell
photographs by Jerry Boucher

Lerner Publications Company • Minneapolis, Minnesota

To Tommy, Elizabeth's rat
—ESP

♡

Thanks to our series consultant, Sharyn Fenwick, elementary science/math specialist. Mrs. Fenwick was the winner of the National Science Teachers Association 1991 Distinguished Teaching Award. She also was the recipient of the Presidential Award for Excellence in Math and Science Teaching, representing the state of Minnesota at the elementary level in 1992.

Ruth Berman, series editor
Steve Foley, series designer

Library of Congress Cataloging-in-Publication Data

Powell, E. Sandy.
    Rats / by E. Sandy Powell ; photographs by Jerry Boucher.
        p. cm.—(Early bird nature books)
    Includes index.
    ISBN 0-8225-3003-1
    1. Rats—Juvenile literature. [1. Rats.] I. Boucher, Jerry, 1941- ill. II. Title. III. Series.
    QL737.R666P68 1994
    599.32'33—dc20   93-40925
                                                         CIP
                                                         AC

Manufactured in the United States of America
1 2 3 4 5 6 – I/SP – 99 98 97 96 95 94

Contents

Be a Word Detective

Can you find these words as you read about the rat's life? Be a detective and try to figure out what they mean. You can turn to the glossary on page 47 for help.

burrows	**molars**	**pups**
colony	**nursing**	**rodents**
grooming	**omnivores**	**scout**
incisors	**predators**	**territory**
litter	**prey**	**weaned**

Chapter 1

A rat can grow to be 10 inches long with a tail that can be as long as 8 inches. Do you think rats make good pets?

Rats, Rats Everywhere

Some people think rats are scary. It's true they can bite. But rats in the wild have loving families. And pet rats can be gentle and friendly. Rats are smart too. In some ways, rats are like people.

Like people, rats can live almost anywhere in the world. They live in crowded cities, on ships, on beaches, on farmland, and in towns. Rats can chew their way into small places, making their homes where larger animals can't bother them.

Rats can chew their way into buildings. They are looking for food or a place to live.

The two main kinds of rats are black rats and brown rats. You can't tell the difference between black and brown rats by their color, though. Not all black rats are black, and not all brown rats are brown. Both kinds of rats can be many colors. They might be gray, reddish brown, white, or almost lavender. You can tell the difference between black and brown rats by their size, shape, and home.

Pet rats are relatives of brown rats. Even though they are called brown rats, they can be many different colors.

The scientific name for brown rats is Rattus norvegicus.
Brown rats make their homes in the ground.

Black rats are smaller than brown rats. But black rats have longer tails. At one time, black rats lived only in trees. Now they also live in attics and on rooftops.

Brown rats are larger than black rats. Still, they can squeeze through spaces only an inch wide. They live underground or in the bottom floors of buildings. Some brown rats live in sewers.

Chapter 2

You can see the four front teeth of the rat who is lying on its back. How long do you think these teeth will grow?

What Is a Rat?

Rats belong to a group of animals called rodents. Mice, squirrels, hamsters, gophers, and beavers are also rodents. Rodents have four front teeth. Two are on the top, and two are on the bottom. These teeth, called incisors (in-SEYE-zurz), are used for gnawing (NAW-ing). The incisors are always growing, just like our fingernails. Rats must gnaw every day to wear down their teeth. When pet rats gnaw on their cages, it looks like they're trying to get out. They may just be taking care of their teeth.

Rats' incisors are always growing. They sometimes gnaw on the bars of their cage to keep their teeth short.

A rat's incisors are sharp and strong. They help rats eat many kinds of food. When rats eat seeds, incisors separate the seeds from the shells. Rats have back teeth called molars. They use their molars for chewing. Rats' lips block the space between the back and front teeth. Their lips keep shells out of their mouth.

These rats are using their incisors to bite into their food.
They use their back molars to chew their food.

Chapter 3

Pet rats eat a mix of seeds, dried fruits, and peanuts. They also love eating fresh fruits and vegetables. Do you think a rat would eat an animal?

Rat Food

Like people, rats are omnivores (AHM-nih-vorz). They eat both plants and animals. Rats eat grains, sugarcane, fruits, and vegetables. They can eat animals such as frogs, lizards, birds, and fish too. They even eat our leftovers. Rats eat many different kinds of food. If one food runs out, rats can switch to eating something else.

Rats need to drink water too. Here two pet rats are drinking water from a bottle.

It might surprise you that rats won't eat spoiled food. They take little bites of strange food. If a rat eats something that makes it sick, other rats know to stay away from that food.

Animals that eat other animals are called predators (PRED-uh-turz). Rats are predators. But rats are prey too. Prey are animals who are eaten by predators. Some of the animals who eat rats are dogs, cats, foxes, skunks, weasels, and otters. Snakes, hawks, and owls eat rats too. Rats live close to their food. If they see a predator, they can quickly scurry home to safety.

If a rat is poisoned and then eaten by a cat, the cat will probably be poisoned too.

Chapter 4

Pet rats dig homes in their bedding. Do you think rats in the wild make different kinds of rooms in their homes?

Homes Underground

 Long ago when people started living in buildings, so did rats. But many brown rats still live underground. Their underground homes are called burrows. Burrows have many rooms. Rats dig out burrows with their noses and front feet. They dig tunnels to connect the rooms.

Like people, rats have rooms for different uses. There are living rooms and eating rooms. Rats also have rooms where they hide from predators and other dangers.

Rats' long, thick whiskers help them feel their way in tight spaces.

There may be 50 to 200 brown rats living together in one burrow. This large group of rats is called a colony. For safety, rats always come out of a burrow headfirst. A rat called the scout leads the way. He stops for a few minutes with his nose out of the hole. This is called testing the wind. The scout is sniffing for enemies. When the scout decides there is no danger, he heads out. Then the other rats know it is safe to follow.

Rats living in a colony are friendly to each other.

Rats move into buildings to stay warm in winter and to be closer to food.

In the winter, it's hard to find enough to eat. So rats may need to move closer to food. They move near people's homes or workplaces. Rats are careful to stay out of sight, though. They hunt for food when it's dark. They also sleep longer in the winter, so they don't need as much to eat.

The scout is checking its territory for enemies. If it senses danger, the scout will make a high-pitched sound that only other rats and some predators can hear.

The area around a colony is called the territory. Rats try to keep strange rats out of their territory. A rat might scare away another rat by clicking its teeth together. Rats also make high-pitched warning sounds. If the new rat doesn't leave, the two rats start bumping noses.

Their tails move back and forth. The rats might also use their teeth to comb each other's fur. They are trying to prove who is stronger. They might nip and bite too. Finally, the two rats stand on their hind legs. They paw at each other, almost like boxers. One rat might attack, biting hard. Usually, the weaker rat gives in before there is an actual fight.

Although these two rats are friends, enemies sometimes comb each other's fur to prove which one is stronger.

Chapter 5

A female rat can have babies up to 10 times a year. What do you think rats make their nests out of?

Babies Are Born

Female rats can begin having babies when they are only three months old. A female rat makes her nest a couple of days before her babies come. She uses twigs, leaves, mattress stuffing, bones, paper, wood chips, almost anything she finds.

This mother rat is having her babies. It takes about an hour and a half for all the babies to be born.

The penny shows how tiny pups are when they are born. Their eyes are closed and they have no hair. Their mother keeps them warm and safe.

These pups are nursing.

Baby rats are called pups. There are usually about nine pups in a litter. A litter is a group of babies who are born together. The pups are born blind, and they have no hair. They depend on their mother for warmth and safety. Pups spend all their time sleeping and nursing. Nursing means drinking mother's milk.

Chapter 6

Hair is just beginning to grow on this pup. Can you guess how old the pup is?

Growing Up

About five days after the pups are born, their hair begins to grow. A few days later, they start to crawl. When a pup crawls out of the nest, the mother carries it back.

Mother rats use their teeth to pick up and carry their pups back to the nest.

The penny shows how much the pups have grown in about two weeks. Now the pups have hair and they can see.

By the end of the second week, the mother rat is tired. The pups can see now, and they begin to roam on their own. If a pup gets too far from its nest, the mother or an older brother or sister helps it back. The father protects the nest from danger. Sometimes, he helps keep the pups warm.

Pups like their brothers and sisters.

An adult rat never uses the nesting area for a bathroom. The mother rat keeps the nest and her pups clean. She cleans her pups with her tongue. This is called grooming. Grooming is

This mother rat is keeping her nest clean by licking her newborn pup.

A rat licks its front feet. Then it cups its toes over its ears down to its nose, over and over again to wash its face clean.

Baby rats learn to use their incisors to comb dirt out of their hair.

one of the first lessons a pup learns. By the time the young rats are two weeks old, they begin to groom themselves.

These baby rats don't need to nurse anymore. They are old enough to eat solid food.

After about three weeks, the pups are weaned. When pups are weaned, they stop nursing and begin eating solid food.

Rats use their front feet to hold their food while they eat.

Young rats learn quickly how to get around. Their tail helps them like an extra arm would help us. A rat's tail is strong. Rats can reach high places by using their tail to push themselves up. Rats stretch their tail out for balance. Black rats wrap their tail around branches or on edges of buildings so they won't fall.

A rat's tail is covered with short hairs. These hairs help the rat feel its way in the dark.

Above: *When climbing, a pet rat uses its tail for balance.*

Left: *A rat's tail is almost like an extra arm.*

35

Chapter 7

Scientists have been studying rats for over 100 years. How long have people been raising rats as pets?

People and Rats

 For over 100 years, scientists have used rats to test medicines and find cures for diseases. People have raised rats as pets for almost 100

years too. When played with every day, the rat becomes a great little buddy. Rats keep themselves clean. They're curious and fun to watch. And they can be held and carried around.

Pet rats are fun to play with and watch.

If you play with it every day, a pet rat can become a good friend.

Here you can see the hole that rats use to get to the grain.
You can also see the droppings rats have left behind.

Wild rats, on the other hand, can be dangerous to people. They bite through electrical wires, gnaw holes in buildings and even in pipes. Wild rats eat and ruin tons of grain each year. They also can carry disease. The diseases can spread to other animals, including us.

In one year, a female rat and her young can give birth to 1,500 rats.

People are one of the reasons there are so many rats in the world today. The buildings we have built give rats more places to live. And we have killed some of the rat's predators, like foxes, weasels, and skunks. More rats can live when they aren't being hunted by predators.

Some dogs are raised for hunting rats.

Like people, rats live in family groups.

Rats are smart, curious, and fun to watch.

Rats and people are alike in some ways. We both live almost anywhere in the world. We both can eat many different kinds of food. And both rats and people live in families. Some things about rats make them easy to like. Other things about rats might make us afraid. But if you get to know a pet rat, you will find out how friendly rats can be.

On Sharing a Book

As you know, adults greatly influence a child's attitude toward reading. When a child sees you read, or when you share a book with a child, you're sending a message that reading is important. Show your child that reading a book together is important to you. Find a comfortable, quiet place. Turn off the television and limit other distractions like telephone calls.

Be prepared to start slowly. Take turns reading parts of this book. Stop and talk about what you're reading. Talk about the photographs. You may find that much of the shared time is spent discussing just a few pages. This discussion time is valuable for both of you, so don't move through the book too quickly. If your child begins to lose interest, stop reading. Continue sharing the book at another time. When you do pick up the book again, be sure to revisit the parts you have already read. Most importantly, enjoy the book!

Be a Vocabulary Detective

You will find a word list on page 5. Words selected for this list are important to the understanding of the topic of this book. Encourage your child to be a word detective and search for the words as you read the book together. Talk about what the words mean and how they are used in the sentence. Do any of these words have more than one meaning? You will find these words defined in a glossary on page 47.

What about Questions?

Use questions to make sure your child understands the information in this book. Here are some suggestions:

> What did this paragraph tell us? What does this picture show? Like people, rats can adapt to their surroundings. For instance, rats can eat whatever food is available. Discuss other ways people and rats adapt. How are rats and people alike and how are they different? Where do brown rats live? Where do black rats live? What is your favorite part of the book? Why?

If your child has questions, don't hesitate to respond with questions of your own like: What do *you* think? Why? What is it that you don't know? If your child can't remember certain facts, turn to the index.

Introducing the Index

The index is an important learning tool. It helps readers get information quickly without searching throughout the whole book. Turn to the index on page 48. Choose an entry, such as *tails,* and ask your child to use the index to find out how rats use their tails. Repeat this exercise with as many entries as you like. Ask your child to point out the differences between an index and a glossary. (The glossary tells readers what words mean, while the index helps readers find information quickly.)

All the World in Metric!

Although our monetary system is in metric units (based on multiples of 10), the United States is one of the few countries in the world that does not use the metric system of measurement. Here are some conversion activities you and your child can do using a calculator:

WHEN YOU KNOW:	MULTIPLY BY:	TO FIND:
miles	1.609	kilometers
feet	0.3048	meters
inches	2.54	centimeters
gallons	3.787	liters
tons	0.907	metric tons
pounds	0.454	kilograms

Family Activities

Visit a pet store and watch pet rats in action. Find out how to care for rats by talking to the people at the store or by reading books from your library.

Visit a zoo or pet store to watch other members of the rodent family. How are they like rats, how are they different?

"Oh, rats!" "You rat!" and "Don't rat on me!" are commonly used expressions. Go to a library and try to find out how these expressions started. Are these expressions fair to rats? Why or why not?

Read several picture books that have rats as characters. How are the rats portrayed? Based on what you've learned in this book, has the rat character been treated fairly? Why or why not?

Help your child write a story about a rat. Use the information from this book to develop the character.

Glossary

burrows—underground homes made by rats

colony—a group of rats living together

gnaw (NAW)—to bite or chew

grooming—cleaning and combing fur

incisors (in-SEYE-zurz)—sharp front teeth used for cutting

litter—a group of babies born at one time

molars—flat teeth used for chewing

nursing—drinking mother's milk

omnivores (AHM-nih-vorz)—animals who eat both plants and animals

predators (PRED-uh-turz)—animals who hunt and eat other animals

prey—animals who are hunted and eaten by other animals

pups—baby rats

rodents—animals who have large front teeth used for cutting

scout—a rat who checks for danger

territory—an area that rats call their own

weaned—to have stopped drinking mother's milk

Index

HUNTINGDON VALLEY LIBRARY

1. Adult periodicals, pamphlets, audio & video cassettes circulate for 1 wk. VIDEOS CANNOT BE RENEWED. All other materials circulate for 3 wks.

2. A fine is charged for each day an item is overdue, except days the library is closed.

3. Each borrower is held responsible for materials charged on his card. All damages and losses shall be paid for at the current market price

GAYLORD F